# Center Of My Mandala

Anuradha Biswas

# Dedication

For all mothers,
who through glaring eyes and clenched teeth,
offer their child a heart full of love,
because they have been there, done that.

# Preface

Mandala is a Sanskrit word meaning 'circle' or 'whole'. It represents the cosmos or the universe. The center of the mandala represents the core of existence. At the core of every mother's existence is her child. The poems in this book trace the life of a mother and her child; from their first words, childhood fears, teenage years to adulthood. The first stanza speaks about the mother, the second stanza about the child. Their worlds are sometimes similar, sometimes varied.  We relive our young life through our children. A mother has been a child once, a child today may be a parent someday. 'Center of my Mandala' is a collection of poems in free verse that celebrate the most natural and beautiful bond in nature: mother and child.

# Acknowledgements

Thank you, to each one of you out there, who have shared their experiences and thoughts with me over the years. This book is a poetic journey inspired by your stories.

# 1. From fofa to sofa

Frocked little girl, a starched pleated woman,
the plump box of dry fruit between them.
'Give it's English name and it is yours', said the woman.
Recall...confusion...remember...frustration...clenched
fists.... 'DATES'
...achievement, as she beat the ants on the pheromone
trail, for a sticky chewy mouthful.
Elite language for elite school admissions.
'Good morning', a look of approval, '*Namaste*', a raised
eyebrow.
Foreign words bouncing off the home's freshly white-
washed walls,
invading conversations like cyborgs in a cybernetic
universe.
The little girl gleefully pouring sand in burnt sienna
cups.


'*Fwing* me on the *fofa*, it won't hurt, it's *foff*'
The frocked girl, a babbling toddler's mother now.
Working on the missing 's', but Grandma likes his '*fofa*'
to 'sofa'.
New country, new ways, new experiences.
Diapers, not cloth nappies ...grandma did not approve.
Native traditions slipping away like Turkish oil

wrestlers.
Grandma implores over the phone
'Another name for DATES?', but '*khejur*' never crosses
the Atlantic.
She makes a note, enroll him in Sunday school.
Roots must grow deep, before they spread wide.

# 2. Palms and Pumpkins

Through the misty paddy fields, walking gingerly on the
narrow ridge;
her long-braided hair like a leash, in Grandpa's hand.
A row of palms, earthen pots dripping with palm sap...
cold, light, sweet.
Few gulps for him, two sips for her.
Pot to pan, the sweet burnt bubbling of jaggery, wafted
through the peeping blossoms on the mango trees.
She crouched, on the unbroken carpet of green,
to see the ducks wade into the pond.
Reflected clouds, rippling under the webbed fleet.
Clouds as frothy, as the milk bucket in the barn.

A cheery hayride under the mellow October sun.
Hugging his mother on the strawy wagon floor.
The pumpkin patch at last, firm mushed smooth warty.
He eyed the autumnal harvest; she looked for pumpkin
flowers,
to make fritters just like her mother did.
Apples on trees, strawberries on the ground;
both waiting to be picked.
Freshly squeezed apple cider, the farm's own ice-cream.
He wanted to feed the ducks, pet the sheep.

She bought tickets; her thoughts resting amidst the palms and ducks.

# 3. Fear

The brightly mosaiced corridors of daytime, hide eerie
creatures in the dark,
To fetch the crayons from the study, a battle plan is
drawn.
Light switches on the way flicked on,
barge in...grab the crayons...dash back...all in one breath.
Summer days are splashed in the pool,
but an unearthly quiet settles as the sun disappears.
She can tame the neighbour's barking Alsatian but not
the silent dark.
The 'Chhau dancers' do not scare her, the intangible
does.
Little feet chase the bees and butterflies, in the
overgrown herb garden;
till fireflies take over, and ghostly eyes wink in the dark.

Red eyed skeletons adorn the front yard,
white flimsy ghosts hang from the barren branches of
the cherry tree.
The coffin door opens every few minutes,
but the boy is unrattled, rather gleeful,
he skips down the street with his load of treats.
She never understood Halloween.
Christmas is her thing...holiday pictures with Santa.

The cherubic old man with ample girth, snowy beard, velvety red robe.
One glance, and the boy's scream sent the elves scurrying.
The gory interests, but peace is disturbing.

# 4. Lunch Break

She tried in vain to follow the teacher,
her borborygmous stomach louder than thunder.
Finally, the lunch bell... books in, colourful lunch boxes
out.
'Pasta' ... seven hungry cupped hands reach out-
a heady mix of marinara, parmesan and ricotta;
not the mustard seed-curry leaves infused macaroni, that
others passed for pasta.
The *rotis* and *parathas* sit ignored;
burgers, *idlis* and *kebabs* quickly disappear.
Mouthfuls of camaraderie, shared flavours,
Food is a great leveller.

Sound of dragging feet, excited conversations.
Uniformly plated lunch trays clanking on cold cafeteria
tables.
Two sliders, sliced apple, baby carrots, chocolate
milkshake.
Two days until Friday...pizza day, he calculates.
Weekend soccer plans discussed between bites.
The last dreg of chocolate milk, then he runs out to play
tag.
Innocent laughter reverberating in the woods,
a metal fence with a clanky gate in between.

The Filipino chased the Korean, the Mexican ran with the Indian;
identity varied, nationality same.

# 5. The Teenaged Mind

try the new anti-acne cream
biology project to be submitted...it's past the deadline
join the drama club in school...or maybe the quiz club
the new young cricketer is cute
ripped jeans look cool...a new nail polish shade
why do we never go on vacation
exams are just two weeks away
learn the lyrics of boyzone's no matter what
hope grandma makes mango pickle this season
'Read the next paragraph', she looked at the teacher
clueless, the class giggled.

air jordan shoes cost too much
library books to be returned...cannot be fined again
mother should enter my room without knocking...
the new girl stays in my neighbourhood... she's pretty
audition for the school play...need tickets for the
Broadway musical
next weekend sleepover in my house
i need to grow facial hair, girls like it
pizza after soccer practice tonight
angling with father is boring, would rather swim
'Your room looks hit by a tornado'.....ignore mother,
headphones back on.

# 6. When the heart flutters

'Loves me, loves me not', her heart racing as the petals
fell.
Beefy boys she would pass, this lean nerd caused a
flutter.
A math problem, a chemical equation, a physics
numerical-
each day she took a new doubt....to watch the sinews in
his arm,
the contraction of his brows, incessant tapping of his
fingers,
a way to accidentally brush his arm; he had blinkers on,
she concluded.
And then the day she still remembers....
ice-cream in hand, he met her at lunchtime.
Long study hours together, stolen moments at the café.
End of high school, the spark fizzled out.

The new girl in ninth grade, with the city girl accent,
a head full of brown curls, a freckled face.
He was on the soccer team, she a cheerleader.
The neighbourhood just became, so much dearer.
Swimming in the lake, cycling in the park,
Walking home, together in the dark.

Mother watched their young hearts bloom,
remembering with a smile the lean nerd in school.
Radiant energy, brimming with ideas, with
tendrils of his dreams growing, wrapped around
mother's love.

# 7. Spring Festivals

Spring green smeared across nature's palette,
delicate winter gardens shrink and wither in the sun.
Winterized pools get ready for a splash,
when the festival of colours comes knocking.
Knocking indeed, with *'bhang'* infused drinks.
Holi... she can be legally high on cannabis.
Boisterous music, intoxicated graceful moves, aimed
water guns.
Her face hidden behind a veil of colours,
dripping puddles as she walks through the house.
A stolen mouthful of fried sweetness from the kitchen.

Store shelves spilling over with colourful egg shells,
candies, ribbons, flowers in pastel shades.
Breakfast with the Easter Bunny...
it excited him once, now he guided children at the table.
The grassy spring air spreading rejuvenation.
Little feet hop run tumble and fall,
filling their vibrant baskets
with the scattered eggs on the grass.
With her years in a convent school, she revered Easter.
For him it was bunnies, eggs and spring break.

# 8. By the Waves

Families descended in hordes on the seaside temple
town,
her troupe of relatives joining the milieu.
Sandy feet jostling for space, among half naked men,
fully clothed women.
The ocean water still warm, from the scorching summer
heat.
Touristy beaches, sound of crashing waves,
subdued under human cacophony.
She longed to be in another place....
In idyllic coastal towns, shores lined with fishing
trawlers,
industrious mornings rolling into leisurely afternoons.
Book, coffee, grilled fish by day; fairy lights, music,
moonlit walks by night.

A row of pristine white houses,
bordering the sandy white beach.
The last weekend before he leaves for college.
Seven friends, young adults, soaking in their freedom.
Breathing in the salty morning air,
sipping the sweet berry smoothie.
The grill ready for the barbeque,
before heading for a swim.

The rhythm of the glistening waves calling.
Funnel cakes and ice-cream on the boardwalk.
Mother made perfect vacation arrangements.

# 9. Cities that breathe

Another muggy afternoon under the mid-summer sun,
the tin roofed taxi trapping the heat like a Dutch oven.
Impatient drivers honking in snail moving traffic.
Hawkers peddling snacks, sun shades, flowers.
She looked at her watch, the movie starts in an hour.
A whiff of jasmine, the riverside flower market.
Windows rolled down, the river breeze blowing her
loose curls away.
Steam boats and motor boats bobbing on the water.
Steeped in history and culture, embracing modernity
Her resilient hometown.

The grey-black-brown of winter gone,
the sidewalk a riot of summery colours and prints.
Museums, zoos, parks bursting at the seams.
Leisurely weekend traffic traversing the streets and
avenues
The lights just coming on, erasing the shadows of
skyscrapers.
He looked up at the dark office windows,
'One day I'll be there, with coffee, bagel, laptop'.
For now, a Broadway show with friends,
before returning home, across the river.
The city an enigma, a Phoenix.

# 10. So long..... Nest

To pack eighteen years in two suitcases.
The line between essentials and non-essentials smudged,
she walked around like a pendulum out of beat.
Bits and pieces of her, scattered around the house,
her bicycle, telescope, the broken doll house, ukulele...
She had longed for independence,
now at it's doorstep, she walked with unsteady steps.
The floral whiffs of incense, the smell of lemony phenyl
on the floor,
clanging of the milk cans every morning, the whistle of
the pressure cooker.
Familiar things left behind, as she stepped into the
unknown.

College campuses visited, decisions made,
applications sent out; response awaited.
Excited chatter with classmates on social media.
Acceptance letter! Celebrations ensued.
With every shirt he packed, a piece of her broke off.
She cried into the pillow, waking up in his empty room.
He longed to go home, to her caramel pudding,
to his father's filter coffee, to them.

Her lonely hours filled with purpose;
volunteering at the local library, guiding young children.

17

# 11. The Accidental Cook

Chop, dice, slice, julienne, mince;
Poached, braised, toasted, sauteed, grilled -
she did not know one from the other.
With a firm glare Grandma set out on her mission;
young girls must know to cook, families are raised in the kitchen.
Vegetables taste best when cooked in their own juices, be patient.
No recipe is an absolute formula, be innovative.
Meat needs to be cooked all the way, be thorough.
Cook pasta al dente, be firm.
Wisdom is found in places other than the classroom.

Open-pour, breakfast of cereal and milk.
Open-assemble, lunch of cheese, bread, prewashed-salad, and dressing.
Open-heat, dinner of frozen pizza and canned soup.
'Boys who can cook slay', mother winked a hint.
Two days of chop, boil, fry, grill, cook... a survival skill for life.
The basics mastered; he tested new recipes at home...
Back in the dorm, the boys snickered.
On the camping trip they had to eat their words;

He made grilled fish and *paella* on the campfire.
They all dug in.

# 12. Am on my Own

She squeezed her eyes shut, hands cupped over her eyes.
Blackout curtains must be hung.
The flimsy satin drape, barely able to keep out the
ferocity of the sun.
The weekend was a blank canvas, waiting to be filled-
laundry, cleaning, groceries, movie.
No assignments, no fixed mealtimes, no queueing up for
the shower.
Tea, newspaper, the hills in the distance, the glimmering
sea beside.
She had to call her parents first, a Sunday ritual.
Every pay check brings with it, fulfilled dreams
The little girl has spread out her wings.

Syrupy pancakes and fried eggs, the kitchen smelled
delicious.
His kitchen, a museum of cardboard boxes;
some spilling onto the dining table and chairs.
Pizza, cereal, pancake mix, dosa mix, cookies, energy
drinks...
'Toss the vegetables with olive oil, salt and pepper',
with that mother hung up, he readied the grill.
A weekend barbeque at the local park,
young men with heavy wallets and swanky cars;

under the California sun.
Mother had taught him well.

21

# 13. Run a Household

Dirty dishes, maid called in sick;
leaking kitchen tap, plumber on vacation;
chair with a broken armrest, carpenter a procrastinator.
Coffee is getting watery, a lactometer to confront the
milkman.
Whites washed with colours again, the careless
washerman.
'Run a household, you can run the country', grandmas
just know.
Her morning allergies are back, ceiling mildew needs
treatment.
There's cooking still to be done....
she slumped on the chair, cup of instant noodles in hand.
With every forkful, regaining an ounce of energy.

The front yard needs work, lawn mower in action;
before a notice from the town council lands in the mail.
Putrid refrigerator- a bag of rotten tomatoes buried
under greens.
'Wipe the walls with vinegar and water',
mother has a home remedy for every problem.
A pile of clothes to be washed, another to be folded.
Vacuum the floors, run the dishwasher, turn on the
garden sprinklers....

Help was one call away- house cleaning services.

In and out in three hours, the house sparkling clean.

The biggest problems may have the easiest solution.

# 14. Loss

Her mind was vacuous,
like an empty crushed soda can,
the empty hospital corridors
through which Grandma's lifeless form passed.
They had dinner together and then …
she was gone… taken away
A heart so full of love,
gave up in one stroke.
She slept on Grandma's bed that night,
among her sarees, she felt her presence.

Holiday plans lay scattered,
in the ashes of a young life snatched unfairly.
Gun wielding maniac, hate crime they said.
Was it the colour of his friend's skin.
He passed by the empty desk in office… why…
Together at the games, at the movies, on the beach…
Apart forever now.
He drove four hours in a trance,
to hug his mother tight,
the embankment of his feelings finally broke.

# 15. Finding Love

The coffee station rendezvous went on for days,
a coincidence first, deliberate later.
From coy smiles, to cafeteria tete-a-tetes.
Lunch hours suddenly seemed short.
She basked in his attention,
office had never felt so idyllic.
Few movie and lunch dates later,
time for the families to meet.
Over cups of tea, fritters and tangy tamarind sauce;
the wedding date was fixed.

Summers spent chasing ice cream trucks together.
Winters in tobogganing down the hill.
Together in high school,
but college put a spanner in the works.
Stolen nights in the mountains,
exploring new places together.
Till he went down on one knee, promise of forever.
Shared days and nights under one roof.
His soul found its mate, they fit like a puzzle,
with dreams of building a life together.

# 16. Wedding Bells

Arms outstretched, she sat in a corner patiently,
intricate henna designs taking shape.
The women danced with abandoned gaiety,
prelude to five days of chaotic celebrations.
She felt buried under the avalanche of relatives.
Weddings - an all expenses paid family reunion.
Under a starry winter sky, glowing in red and gold,
her hand was placed in his, amidst echoes of holy
chanting.
Their bond of love forged by the sacred fire, marked by
the vermillion.
Moist eyes followed her; leaving one home to build
another.

They planned a sunset beach wedding,
close circle of friends and family in attendance.
Bridal shower and bachelorette parties taken care of.
Pastels was the colour of all wedding finery.
He wrote his vows, so did she, holy chanting kept
minimal.
With a soft proud look, mother blessed them.
As the sacred fire rose up, to match the colour of the
setting sun,
they were united in bonds of love and trust.

The smell of fresh flowers, the sea spray, the copper glow in the sky,
lulled the senses as a new chapter opened in his life.

# 17. Joy

Her morning alarm went off, his side of the bed was empty.
Subdued rattle of pots and pans, slow whistling of the kettle.
A hug and a lingering kiss amidst the aroma of Darjeeling tea, a sleeping baby.
The joy of waking up to a cup of steaming tea...wedded bliss.
A hustled-up breakfast; the car delivery scheduled at noon.
A drive by the sea in their new four-wheeler,
not rented...not borrowed...not gifted...bought with their savings.
Feeding the baby, pouring over home loan paperwork,
looking for a nanny, haggling with the local vendors...
The joy of it all, with him beside her.

The nutty aroma of freshly brewed coffee, his morning alarm.
On the yoga mat, her body twisted in a triangle pose.
Accustomed to the randomness of his bachelor life,
this rhythmic wedded existence was a novelty.
He walked the dog, she ran the garden sprinklers,
he got breakfast going, she packed sandwiches for lunch,

he dropped off the baby at daycare, she did the pick-up.
Returning every night to a warm meal, a loving wife, a
babbling baby;
his precious little world ... as he was his mother's.
'Mother, come and stay with us for some time', he urged.

# 18. Hello Neighbour

Human minds have conditional alignment, changing
loyalties;
with relation among neighbours, more volatile than nail
polish removers.
Her neighbours ranged from thirty to eighty,
myriad temperaments, harmony at times hanging,
by a thread more delicate than a soap bubble.
The narcissists were dreaded and avoided, so were their
sycophants.
The pseudo-intellectuals' best ally was Google.
The sassy sixty-year-olds had just found their wings.
The wise listened and observed; the wiser kept to
themselves.
The grannies walked around with a 'we have seen it all'
smile.

Trees sprouting new leaves, front yards vibrant with
spring blooms,
backyard pools and trampolines set up.
The neighbourhood waking up from its winter slumber.
Winter house parties to summer barbeques;
a vibrant community of well-heeled immigrants.
The McCarthys led the St. Patrick's Day parade.
The Jones' did the Easter egg hunt, pitter-patter of tiny

feet in the park.

He organised Holi, a colourful rain dance with garden sprinklers.

The gun shots at the local primary school shattered it all....

The nine-year-old shooter lived two houses down the street.

# 19. The Mother

The soup simmered on the stovetop,
She buttered the bread, mixed the salad.
Her husband stood at the doorway watching.
'Let us go home'.
Through laughter and tears they kissed.

Wrapping up thirty years in three months.
Their son took some time, but understood.
At sixty, seeking a new journey to an old destination.
The longing in their heart, to leave
the land they called home, for that which was always
home.

She felt like she had never gone away.
The same wispy autumn clouds, start of the festive
season.
Her city shining bright with Diwali lights.
Pampered by maids, cook, driver.
She soaked in familiar sounds, sights, tastes of her
beloved hometown.

Her husband raided the local fish market.
She fluttered like a butterfly, among family and friends.
Her existence twined around snippets from the past,

and hopes for the future.

But the centre of her existence was across the Atlantic.

# 20. The Son

Snowflakes whirled around before settling;
coating cold surfaces, melting on the warm car hood-
still warm from the airport trip.
He suddenly felt orphaned.
Four hours drive to fourteen hours trans-Atlantic flight.

Weekend visits, turned annual.
He stood by the window watching,
his five-year-old scooping up the snow in excitement.
The neighbourhood turned white,
all forms and colours disappearing into an undulating
landscape.

The repetitive rhythm of everyday living,
lulled his spirit of adventurous exploration.
Seeing his parents take off a year ago,
rippled the calm surface of his existence.
The spark now rekindled, zest for life restored.

'Let us go home. Take up the offer'......
his wife, his rock, his mind reader.
Two years to explore his roots.
The joy in mother's choked voice, the excitement in his.
Salt and pepper go together.

# 21. Center of my Mandala

Soft as an avocado, hard as a coconut.
Deceptive comparisons.
The centre matters, the source.
Her yielding nature, around a resolute core.
His hardy demeanour, a compassionate soul.
Forests grow back greener after a fire,
the ash making the seed grow stronger.
She retraced her journey with every step he took;
he learnt from each observation she made.
Mother and child ... each the other's life source.

The center of his being - mother,
his biggest cheerleader, his harshest critic.
Ripples of time reaching the shores of a timeless bond
pulling her away, he clings, she slips from his grasp.
A wave of recollections washes over his hollow core,
filling the void with hope, strength, and dreams for
tomorrow.
Spring leaves on barren branches erasing the memory of
winter,
summer's rich foliage, turns fiery red in autumn.
Leaves come and go, the tree stands rooted.
My tree, my mother, the center of my mandala.